REVELATIONS OF THE AFTERLIFE

Revelations of the Afterlife

A New Arrival

SHIRLEY SMOLKO

W. T. Stead

Cavallaro Publishing

CONTENTS

~ twenty-three ~
Spiritualist Beliefs About the Afterlife
80

Revelations of the Afterlife: A New Arrival

Copyright © 2022 by Shirley Smolko

Printed in the U.S.A.

First Printing, 2022

Second Printing, 2023

ISBN: 978-1-958104-04-0

Library of Congress Control Number: 2022907823

Cavallaro Publishing
North Venice, Florida
www.cavallaropub.com
cavallaropub@gmail.com

DISCLAIMER

Although I have attempted to make the original text of *The Blue Island* more gender-sensitive, it is still a product of a distant time and could contain some gender-insensitive material that may have been missed in the edit. Therefore, all pronouns shall be deemed to refer to the masculine, feminine, neuter, singular, or plural; wherever used herein, a pronoun in the masculine gender shall be considered to include the feminine gender. I have also taken out much of the archaic language and rewritten some sentences or paragraphs in an effort to promote clarity.

PREFACE

As the title implies, *Revelations of the Afterlife* contains revelations about the afterlife from two different spirit entities separated by time, space, and culture. The first story comes from the book *The Blue Island: Experiences of a New Arrival Beyond the Veil*. It was channeled through Psychic Medium Pardoe Woodman and is about the experiences of William T. Stead, who, along with hundreds of others, drowned in the icy waters of the North Atlantic upon the sinking of the Titanic.

Ten years later, Mr. Stead's daughter, Estelle, published his communication from the other side. In the book, Mr. Stead describes his death at sea and the nature of the afterlife. The manuscript of *The Blue Island* was produced using automatic writing.

In the following excerpt, he describes the tragic scene he witnessed upon his passing:

> In a matter of a few minutes in time only, there were hundreds of bodies floating in the water—dead—hundreds of souls carried through the air, alive; very much alive... The scene on the boat at the time of the sinking was not so pleasant, but it was nothing compared to the scene among the poor souls newly thrust out of their bodies, all unwillingly. It was both heartbreaking and repellent. And thus we waited, waiting until all were collected until all were ready, and then we moved our scene to a different land.

In an attempt to improve the readability and comprehension of the first story from the book, *The Blue Island,* I have made significant changes by rewriting some sentences and paragraphs or by completely omitting those that were confusing, redundant, or extraneous in nature. Archaic words have been replaced with modern expressions, and I have also attempted to replace gender-specific pronouns with gender-neutral ones.

The second story is an excerpt from one of my books, *Just a Thought Away: Communicating With Loved Ones in Spirit.* It is a revelation of the afterlife given to me during a dream by my tour guide, teacher, and fellow light worker—Paolo. My fascinating journey begins in the hellish realms of the abyss and ends in the magnificent planes of heaven.

One night, after retiring to bed, I asked God to show me the world of Spirit. During readings, I had seen glimpses of the afterlife for as long as I could remember, but I had a deep desire for a better understanding. I felt it would help give me insight into the condition and state of existence of the spirits I delivered messages for. Soon after falling asleep, I began a tour of the spirit world that would forever impact my perspective on the afterlife. I am very excited to have the opportunity to share this tour with you!

Shirley Smolko—The Venetian Medium

Part One: The Blue Island

A Word From the Channeled Spirit of W. T. Stead

The Channeled Book

The Arrival

The Blue Island

Interesting Buildings

Life on the Island

Intimate Life

More About Intimate Life

~ One ~

A WORD FROM THE CHANNELED SPIRIT OF W. T. STEAD

In earth life, I did my best to help enlighten others about the afterlife, but I was very restricted owing to material calls upon my time. Since my arrival in this land, I have tried to carry on and greatly increase the amount and scope of the same work. I have succeeded up to a point, though many have not yet reached the halfway point on that staircase of knowledge leading to understanding. I was on the point of saying that it *leads to happiness*, but that would not be quite correct, for happiness is most amply contained in *understanding*, and happiness in the sense that it is used and understood on earth is *not the raison d'etre (reason for existence)* of life. We were not made to be happy. Happiness is part of our reward for work done, for progress, and for help given to others—which is itself the outcome of understanding.

As I have said, in my work on this side of the Borderland I have achieved a certain success, and I am confident that if I can pass on the knowledge I have gained, together with my own personal experiences, to you who are still on earth, I shall have gone a little farther in the work to which I have set my hand for the good of humanity.

What I have to say will be of interest to many and useless to many more, but I am going to say things that each one of my readers can, up to a point, test for themselves. You can each test it by your soul knowledge, and by that, you will know that I am giving you words of value, words that God, in His infinite love, has permitted me to be the means of passing on to you. It is not *my* idea of the mysteries of life; it is a discourse on those mysteries.

There is the teaching of Christianity running through it all, but the application is different from that ordinarily accepted. It is quite erroneous to suppose that because someone was a man or woman on earth, they will become a spirit the moment they die because they are already a spirit. Death is only the doorway from one room to another, and both rooms are very similarly furnished and arranged. That's what I want you to appreciate thoroughly; it is under the same guiding hand. The same Personality rules in all spheres.

Beginning at the beginning, I have to tell you how someone finds themselves here on arrival. As I have said, this whole book will interest many and help a few. It is for those few that all concerned are making the necessary effort to bring it to them. It does not attempt or pretend to be scientific.

I must impress upon you all—the interested and the disinterested, the believer in this great subject, Spiritualism, and the skeptic—to remember you are still on earth and you still have to perform earth's duties. You have your daily lives to lead, and you must always do the work at hand well. Never neglect the present because the future appears more brightly colored. Carry on with today, but with a corner of your mind on tomorrow, and remember also that Spiritualism is *not* for everyone.

William T. Stead.

~ Two ~

THE CHANNELED BOOK

When, in April 1912, the *Titanic* sank in mid-ocean and my father passed on to the next world, I was on tour with my own Shakespearean Company. Among the members of that Company was a young man named Pardoe Woodman, who, on the very Sunday of the disaster, foretold it as we sat talking after tea. He did not name the boat or my father, but he got so much that pointed to disaster at sea and the passing on of an elderly man intimately connected with me that when the sad news came through, we realized he must have been closely in touch with what was about to happen. I mention this incident because it formed the first link between my father and Mr. Woodman, and as it is largely due to Mr. Woodman's psychic powers that my father has been able to get through the messages that are contained in this book, I think it will be of interest to readers and should be put on record.

Two weeks after the disaster, I saw my father's face and heard his voice just as distinctly as I heard it when he bade me good-bye before embarking on the Titanic. This was at a sitting with Etta Wriedt, the well-known American direct voice medium. At this sitting, I talked with my father for over twenty minutes. This may seem like an amazing assertion to many, but it is a fact vouched for by all those who were present at the sitting. I put it on record at the time in an article published in *Nash's Magazine,* which included the signed testimonies of all those present.

From that day to this, I have been in constant touch with my father. I have had many talks with him, and communications from him contain very definite proof of his continued presence among us. I can truly say that the link between us is even stronger today than it was in 1912, when he threw off his physical body and passed on to the spirit world. There has never been a feeling of parting, although at first the absence of his physical presence was naturally a source of great sadness.

In 1917, Mr. Woodman was discharged from the Army due to an injury and came to stay with us at our country cottage at Cobham. While with us, the news came to him that his great friend had been killed at the front, and his interest in the possibility of communication with the next world, which had been indifferent till then, became intense, and he set out to find out for himself. It is always the passing of a loved one that gives the necessary stimulus for eager inquiry.

It was not long before his friend was able to give him definite proof of his continued existence and his ability to communicate. His first proofs were given through Vout Peters and were followed by others through Gladys Osborne Leonard's mediumship and through the mediumship of friends gifted with psychic powers. I was present at that first sitting with Mr. Peters; my father was there also, and his friend said it was due to my father's presence and help that he was able to succeed so well in these first attempts at communication. Shortly after this, Mr. Woodman found that he himself had the power of automatic writing, and his father and others were soon able to write through him. Father always prefers me to be present, as if I am not, he seems to have more difficulty and very rarely attempts to write. He explains the necessity of my presence in this way: he and I are so much *in rapport* and so closely in touch with each other that he is able to draw much power from me; I act as the connecting link and form a sort of battery between him and Mr. Woodman. I merely sit passively by while Mr. Woodman Writes. Certainly, I see a light around us and a strong ray of light concentrating on Mr. Woodman's arm. Sometimes I am able to see Father himself, and always, when he is writing, I feel his presence very distinctly.

We have received many messages in this way. For a while in 1918, we sat regularly every week, were kept in touch with much that was going on at the Front and about what was about to happen, and were advised of occurrences often days before the news came through in an ordinary way. In one case, Father gave us the actual headlines that would (and did) appear in the papers the following week.

It is also interesting and important to note that Mr. Woodman and my father met only once before the latter's passing. I introduced Mr. Woodman to him not long before he left England on the *Titanic,* and they only exchanged two or three words. Therefore, Mr. Woodman never knew my father personally, nor has he come into contact with his writings or with his work in any way, and yet the wording and the phrasing of the messages are my father's, and even the manner of writing is typical of him.

Mr. Woodman also writes with his eyes closed and often holds a handkerchief over them. Some of the best messages were given in the twilight, when it was impossible for me to follow what was being written, and yet the words were never overwritten. The writing will stop sometimes while my father evidently reads over what has been written, and alterations will be made, i's dotted, and t's crossed correctly. It was a habit of my father's, while here, to go back over his copy and cross his t's and dot his i's; this habit was only known to a few and was certainly absolutely unknown to Mr. Woodman.

Two of the messages obtained in this way have already been published. They were given by my father for Armistice Day, 1920, and Armistice Day, 1921. First, we had no idea he contemplated giving a message. A few friends, including Mr. Woodman, were taking tea with my mother and me on the Sunday before the 11th of November. We had been chatting on various subjects when I suddenly felt my father come into the room. I could tell by the feeling he gave me that he wished we would give him an opportunity to write and that it was urgent. It was impossible to arrange for that evening, so we made an appointment for the following evening. Mr. Woodman came about nine o'clock. We sat chatting by the fire for a few minutes; then we felt Father come in, and we sat at once. Father's manner was exactly as it used to be when here in the body, and he wanted to get something important done. He must concentrate on that and nothing else. Directly as we sat, Mr. Woodman's hand began to move, and my father wrote words to this effect: "I have my message ready, and if you do not interrupt, I hope to succeed in getting it through." He wrote at tremendous speed and, in about half an hour, had given his message. Having finished, he gave directions that it should be read through and punctuated, if necessary. Then he left us, not saying a word about anything else. It was a strenuous half hour for us all, but it was worth it. The message was printed the next day, and many thousands were distributed to those visiting the Cenotaph that year. The 1921 message was given in the same manner, and thousands of copies of the two messages, now printed in pamphlet form, were distributed on Armistice Day, 1921.

It was soon after giving this last message that Father expressed the wish that we should sit for the messages given in this book. We had felt for some time that he was wanting us to sit for a series of messages but asked that if this were so, he would give us definite instructions to this effect from an outside source. This he did by asking Mrs. Kelway Bamber, the author of "Claude's Books," at a sitting, which she was having with Mrs. Leonard, to tell us that it was quite true that he did wish us to sit for a series of messages, which he said would tell of his arrival and some of his experiences on the Other Side.

Both Mr. Woodman and I are busy people and can only give what spare time we have from our ordinary work to psychic matters, so it was difficult to fit in times; therefore, it was a few months before we had finished taking the messages. These were all given in the manner already described. They were consecutive, but definite instructions were not given as to how the whole series was to be arranged.

Father's foreword explains his object in writing this book, so there is no need to dwell on that here. When he started, he had a rather longer book in mind, but decided in favor of a short book, as it is more likely to be read, can be published at a reasonable price, and so stands the chance of reaching more people. All who worked with my father here will know that such reasoning was characteristic of him.

The photograph given as the frontispiece to this volume (on the original book cover) was taken by the Crewe Circle at Crewe in the autumn of 1915. In the spring of that year, I had met Mr. Hope and Mrs. Buxton at the house of a mutual friend in Glasgow, and they very kindly invited me to call and see them in Crewe if I should ever have an opportunity to do so. Soon after my return to London, my father asked me to arrange to go to Crewe, as he said he wanted to try to give us his picture on the same plate as mine. Accordingly, I arranged to spend a weekend with some friends at Crewe and have some sittings with Mr. Hope and Mrs. Buxton.

I bought a box of photographic plates in London and took them with me, and I can truthfully say that that box of plates never left my sight or my possession all the time I was there. I even slept with the box clasped tightly in my hands. We had our first sitting on Saturday, when I obtained two extras, neither resembling my father. One was of interest because it was the picture of a lady who had appeared on a plate with my father when he was experimenting with Mr. Boursnell in the 'nineties (1890s). I took my box containing the rest of the plates away with me after the sitting, bought another box of plates in Crewe, and took both boxes with me to the sitting on Sunday. We did not use my first box at all at this sitting, and I kept it all the while just inside my dress. We sat around the table, putting our hands over and under the second box for a few minutes. I then held the box for a minute against Mrs. Buxton's forehead. After this, I was instructed by Mr. Hope's guide to take the box myself into the dark room (note that the box had not been unsealed or the plates exposed to the light).

When in the dark room, I was to unseal the box and take out the two bottom plates, taking particular care to note which was the bottom plate, and then to develop both plates. Mr. Hope was to come in with me but not touch the box or plates. I followed the instructions. I found the bottom plate not even fogged, and on the other plate two messages: one from Archdeacon Colley, deploring my father's inability to write; one from Mr. Walker, the father of my host; and in one corner of the plate a faint outline of my father's face.

When I got back to my friends that evening, we had a sitting at which my father expressed his keen disappointment at his failure to give his picture. "It is all my fault", he said. "I am so excited at the idea of getting my picture beside yours after I have been so-called 'dead' for so many years that I break the conditions; however, many have promised to help me tomorrow, and if I fail again, we have something else prepared to slip on so that you will not be disappointed."

On the following morning, I went for my last sitting. Two of my own plates were used. Both of these are pictures of my father; one is reproduced in this book, and the other is a large face of my father that completely covers me.

Now, having—I hope—given a little idea as to how these messages were obtained and our reasons for feeling that they do indeed come from my father, I am content to let *The Blue Island* do the rest. I am sure it will interest many, and if it awakens some to a truer realization of what is to come and makes them seek for further definite proofs themselves, then the three chiefly concerned in giving these messages to the public—my father, Mr. Woodman, and myself—will be amply satisfied.

Estelle W. Stead
September 1922

~ Three ~

THE ARRIVAL

M any years ago, I was attracted by an article on the subject of spirit communication, and, after reading it carefully several times, I was forced to admit its soundness. I was struck by the plain and practical ideas of the writer. This was the first reason I became actively interested in this big and amazing work. From that time on, I did all in my power to prove and then forward the movement. Many people know this, and those who do not can become acquainted with the details if they wish. Therefore, I am going to pass at once from my first interest in the occult to my first interest in the earth.

While on Earth, I was overcome with astonishment and satisfaction at first reaching my convictions about life after death. I was even more astonished upon coming to this land and finding that my knowledge of the afterlife, which I gained on Earth, was strikingly correct in nearly all the chief points. There was great satisfaction in proving this. I was at once amazed and delighted to find so much truth in all I had learned, for although I had believed implicitly, I was not entirely without grave misgivings about many minor details. Hence my general satisfaction when I recognized things and features that, though I had accepted them while on earth, I had scarcely anticipated would be as I now found them. This must sound somewhat contradictory, but I want you to understand that my earthly misgivings were based on the fear that perhaps the spirit world had a formula of its own that was quite different from our earthly mentality and that, therefore, the many points were transmitted to us in such a form and in such expression as we on earth would be able to grasp and appreciate and were not in themselves precise descriptions, owing to the limitations of earthly word-expression.

Of my actual passing from earthly life to spirit life, I do not wish to write more than a few lines. I have already spoken of it several times and in several places. The first part of it was naturally an extremely discordant one, but from the time my physical life ended, there was no longer a sense of struggling with overwhelming odds, but I do not wish to speak of that.

My first surprise came when—I now understand that, to your way of thinking, I was dead—I found I was in a position to help people. From being in dire straits myself to being able to lend a hand to others, it was such a sudden transition that I was frankly and blankly surprised. I was so taken aback that I did not consider the why or the wherefore at all. I was suddenly able to help. I did not know how or why, and I did not attempt to inquire. There was no analysis then; that came a little later.

I was also surprised to find several friends with me—people I knew had passed over years before. That was the first reason I realized the change had taken place. I knew it suddenly and was a trifle alarmed. Practically instantaneously, I found myself looking for myself. Just a moment of agitation, momentary only, and then the full and glorious realization that all I had learned was true. Oh, how badly I needed a telephone at that moment. I felt I could give the papers some headlines for the evening. That was my first realization; then came helplessness—a reaction—a thought of all my own at home—they didn't know yet. What would they think of me? Here I was, with my telephone out of working order for the present. I was still so close to the earth that I could see everything going on there. Where I was, I could see the wrecked ship, the people, and the whole scene, and that seemed to pull me into action—I could help. And so in a few seconds—though I am now taking a long time to tell you, it was only a few seconds really—I found myself changed from a helpless state to one of action—*helpful,* not helpless.

The end came, and it was all finished. We waited until the disaster was complete. The saved are saved, and the dead are alive. Then, as a group, we moved our scene. It was a strange method of traveling for us all, and we were a strange crew, bound for a place we did not know where. The whole scene was indescribably pathetic. Many, knowing what had occurred, were in agony of doubt as to their people left behind and as to their own future state. What would it hold for them? Would they be taken to see Him (God)? What would their sentence be? Others were almost mental wrecks. They knew nothing; they seemed uninterested in everything; their minds were paralyzed. A strange crew indeed of human souls waiting for their ratings in the new land

In a matter of a few minutes, there were hundreds of bodies floating in the water and hundreds of souls carried through the air. Many, realizing their death had come, were enraged at their powerlessness to save their valuables. They fought to save what they valued so much on earth.

The scene on the boat at the time of the strike was not so pleasant, but it was nothing compared to the scene among the poor souls newly thrust out of their bodies, all unwillingly. It was both heartbreaking and repellent. And thus we waited—waited until all were collected and all were ready, then we moved our scene to a different land.

It was a curious journey. Far more strange than anything I had anticipated. We seemed to rise vertically into the air at terrific speed. As a whole, we moved as if we were on a very large platform, and this was hurled into the air with gigantic strength and speed, yet there was no feeling of insecurity. We were quite steady. I cannot tell how long our journey lasted or how far from the earth we were when we arrived, but it was a gloriously beautiful arrival. It was like walking under your own Indian Sky. There was brightness and beauty. We saw this land far off when we were approaching, and those of us who could understand realized that we were being taken to the place destined for all those people who pass over suddenly—on account of its general appeal. It helps the nerve-racked newcomer fall into line and regain mental balance very quickly. We arrived feeling, in a sense, proud of ourselves. It was all lightness and brightness. Everything was as physical and quite as material in every way as the world we had just finished with.

Our arrival was greeted with welcomes from many old friends and relatives who had been dear to each of us in our earthly lives. And having arrived, the people who had come over from that ill-fated ship parted company. We were free agents again, though each one of us was in the company of some personal friends who had been over here a long time.

~ Four ~

THE BLUE ISLAND

I have told you a little about my journey and arrival, and now I want to tell you my first impression and a few experiences. I must begin by saying I do not know how long after the collision these experiences took place. It seemed to be a continuation without any break, but I cannot be certain that this was so.

I found myself in the company of two old friends, one of whom was my father. He came to be with me, to help, and to show me around. It was like arriving in a foreign country and having a buddy to go around with. That was the principal sensation. The scene from which we had so recently come was already well relegated to the past. Having accepted the change of death, all the horror of our late experience had gone. It might have been fifty years ago instead of, perhaps, only last night. Consequently, our pleasure in the new land was not marred by grief at being parted from earthly friends. I will not say that none were unhappy; many were, but that was because they did not understand the nearness of the two worlds; they did not know what was possible, but to those who understood the possibilities, it was in a sense the feeling, *Let us enjoy a little of this new land before returning our thoughts to our earthly home,* and therefore there was little grief in our arrival.

In writing about my first experiences, I am going to give a certain amount of detail. My old sense of humor is still with me, I am glad to say, and I know that what I have to say now will cause a certain amount of amusement to those who treat this subject lightly, but I do not mind. I am glad they will find something to smile at— it will make an impression on them that way, and then when their own time comes for the change, they will recognize themselves amongst the conditions of which I am going to write. Therefore, to that kind of skeptic, I just say, "It's all right, friend," and "You give no offense."

My father and I, along with my friend, set out immediately. A curious thing struck me. I was clothed exactly as I had been, and it seemed a little strange to me to think I had brought my clothing with me! There's number one, Mr. Skeptic!

My father was also dressed as I had always known him. Everything and everybody appeared to be quite normal, as on Earth. We went out together and had refreshments at once, and naturally, that was followed by much discussion about our mutual friends on both sides. I told them about my experiences on Earth, and they told me about life in this new country as compared to Earth.

Another thing that struck me was the general coloring of the place; in England, it would be difficult to say what the impression of coloring is, but I suppose it would be considered grey-green. Here there was no uncertainty about the impression; it is undoubtedly a blue that predominated. A light shade of blue. I do not mean the people, trees, houses, etc. were all blue, but the general impression was that of a blue land.

I commented upon this to my father—who, by the way, was considerably more active and younger than he was at the time of his death; we looked more like brothers. I spoke of this impression of blue, and he explained that it was so in a sense. There was a great predominance of blue rays in the light, and that was why it was such a wonderful place for mental recovery. Now some say, "How completely foolish!" Well, have you not experienced certain places on earth considered especially good for this or that ailment? Then bring common sense to bear and realize that the next step after death is only a very small one. You do not go from indifferent man-hood to perfect godliness! It is not like that; it is all progress and evolution, and as with people, so with the land. The next world is only a complement to the present one.

We were a small population in that country. There were People of all conditions, of all colors, of all races, and of all sizes; all went about freely together, but there was a great sense of caring only for oneself—self-absorption. A bad thing on earth, but a necessary thing here, both for the general and individual good. There would be no progress or recovery in this land without it. As a result of this absorption, there was a general peace among these many people, and this peace would not have been attained without this self-centeredness. No one took notice of any others. Each stood for himself and was almost unaware of all the others.

There were not many people I knew. Most of those who came to meet me had disappeared again, and I saw scarcely any I knew except my two companions. I was not sorry for this. It gave me a better chance of appreciating all the new scenes before me. There was the sea where we were, and I and my companions went for a long walk together along the shore. It was not like one of your seaside resorts, with promenades and bands; it was a peaceful and lovely spot. There were some very big buildings on our right, and on our left was the sea. All was light and bright, and again, this blue atmosphere was very marked. I do not know how far we went, but we talked incessantly of our new conditions and of my own folk at home and of the possibility of letting them know how it fared with me, and I think we must have gone a long way. If you can imagine what your world would look like if it were compressed into a place, say, the size of England—with some of all people, all climates, all scenery, all buildings, and all animals—then you can perhaps form an idea of this place I was in. It must all sound very unreal and dreamlike, but, believe me, it was only like being in a foreign coun-try and nothing else, except that it was absorbingly interesting.

I want to give you a picture of this new land without going too deeply into the minute details. We arrived at length at a huge building, circular and with a great dome. Its general appearance was that of a dome only—on legs—a great dome supported on vast columns, circular and very big. Again, in the interior, it was an amazingly lovely blue. It was not a fantastic structure in any way. It was just a beautiful building, as you have on earth—do not imagine anything fairylike; it was not. This blue was again very predominant, and it gave me a feeling of energy. I wanted to write immediately. I would have liked to have been a poet at that moment, but as it was, I just wanted to express myself with pen and paper.

We stayed there some time and had refreshments very similar, it seemed to me, to what I had always known on Earth, only there was no fresh food. Everything appeared quite normal there, and the absence of some things that would on earth have been present was not noticed. The curious thing was that the meal did not seem at all a necessity—it was there, and we all partook of it lightly, but it was more from habit than need—and I seemed to draw much more strength and energy out of the atmosphere itself. This I attributed to the color and air. It was while we were in this place that my father explained the purpose and work of the different buildings I had noted on our walk together.

~ Five ~

INTERESTING BUILDINGS

L ooked upon as a meal—a lunch out—it was the longest one I
have ever known and without question the most interesting. I
learned a great deal in those first few hours with my father. It was
all conversational, but it was of great use to me and of vast interest.
He explained to me that the place we were then in was a temporary
rest house, one of many, but the one most used by newly-arrived
spirit people. It was closest to earthly conditions and was used
because it resembled an earthly place in appearance. There were
other buildings used for the same purpose as well as for other
purposes; by that, I mean there was more than *one* of each.

These houses were not all alike; they varied considerably in
outward appearance, but there is no need to describe each. To call
it a big building is sufficient, and by that, you must understand a
place like your museum, your portrait gallery, or your large hotels.
anything you like, and it is near enough. But it was not fantastic in
any way and had no peculiarities; therefore, by building," I mean
a building only. There were a great number of these places in
different parts—not grouped together, but variously placed about
this land.

It seems that all the senses are provided for here. The chief work
on this island is to get rid of unhappiness at parting from earthly
ties, and therefore, for the time being, the individual is allowed to

indulge in most of the earth's pleasures. There are attractions of all kinds to stimulate and, generally, tone up strength. Whatever the person's particular interest on earth has been, he can follow it up and indulge in it here as well for the present. All mental interests and almost all physical interests can be continued here for the simple reason of coaxing the newcomer to a level of mental outlook.

There are houses given over to book study, music, and athleticism of all kinds. Every kind of physical game can be practiced—you can ride on horseback, you can swim in the sea. You can have any kind of sport that does not involve the taking of a life. In a minor degree, that can be had too, but not in reality; that is only make-believe.

From this, you will understand that particular buildings are given over to their own kind of work. The man who has spent his life in games, heart, and soul would be disconsolate without them here. He can have them and enjoy them to the full, but he will find that after a time the desire is not so keen, and he will turn to other interests automatically, though gradually. It may be that he will never entirely abandon his games, but the desire will be less absorbing. On the other hand, the man who used his life for, say, music, for instance, will find his desire, his interest, and his ability increasing by leaps and bounds—because music belongs to this land. He will find that by spending much time in one of the music houses, as he *will* if his life is music, his knowledge and abilities are amazingly increased. Then there is the bookworm. He, too, finds intense satisfaction in his new-found facilities. Knowledge is unlimited—works of priceless value, lost upon earth, are in existence here. He is provided for.

The keenest businessman on earth whose only interest is in making his business successful will also find scope for ability. He will come into contact with the house of organization, and he will find himself linked up with work that transcends in interest anything that he could have imagined for himself while upon the earth.

All this is done for a reason. Everyone is provided for. On arriving here, there is often much grief, grief that is sometimes incapacitating, and no movement forward can be made until the individual wishes it himself. Progress cannot be forced on him. Thus, in the scheme of creation, the blessed Creator has devised this wonderful means of appealing to the main interest on earth of each one. Everyone comes in touch with the chief longing of earthly life and is given the opportunity to indulge in it; thus, progress is assured.

In all things that are purely and solely of the earth, the interest weakens after a little time; it is a gradual process—nothing is dramatic here—and the person passes from this to another interest, which on earth would be called a mental one. Those whose interests have been in this category will continue to expand the scope of their work and will progress along the same lines as the others.

While on this Blue Island, each one is very much in touch with the conditions left behind. At first, there is nothing done but what is both helpful and comforting—later, there is a refining process to be gone through. At first, it is possible to be closely in touch with the home left behind, but after a little time, there is a reaction from this desire to be so close to the earth, and when that sets in, the process of eliminating earth and flesh instincts begins. In each case, this takes a different course and a different length of time.

In trying thus to explain the use of this land and its buildings, I have not numbered them "Building A" for so-and-so, "Building B" for this, that, and the other, but, in a conversational way, I hope I have helped you to understand and form a general idea of this country and some of its conditions. I hope I have made it clear now that, after a time, the desire for earthly things leaves us all. It may be a short or long time, according to the disposition of the person concerned. Take the athlete. He loves his games, his running, his physical strength, and his muscular exercise. Well, he will love it here just as much. He will love it here more because he will find an added pleasure in feeling no fatigue, a sharpened enjoyment altogether, but after a time, his appreciation of all this will change.

He will not dislike this beloved sport, but he will prefer a different form of it. A form that is full of movement and satisfaction but not a physical affair at all; his mind will become more awake, and he will get enormous mental satisfaction from the studies that will come before him concerning the ways and means of travel here. Locomotion of all kinds here is very different to that which obtains in earthly conditions, and this former athlete of the earth will drop into line in his new surroundings and will presently realize that life here is a different thing for him, for, though still on the same lines, it holds an increased mental interest. Is that clear? Well, apply it in the same fashion to every other type of individual.

~ Six ~

LIFE ON THE ISLAND

Having given you a little idea of this land and its appearance, I want to tell you about the lives of the people here so that you can form a complete mental picture. It is only natural that many should say, "What are they all doing?" Now, this is a very broad question to answer, and to help you see how big a thing I am dealing with in attempting to tell my story of the next life, I must paint you a picture.

I want you to try to imagine that you are an alien from a faraway planet. Knowing nothing of earthly life, you have suddenly landed by airship in the busiest part of the city of London—with all its traffic and people. You have arrived from some other world and have not seen Earth before. You will exclaim, "How strange. What are they all doing?" Well, could you answer that question easily? It would not mean much to you to be told they are going about their own individual businesses—one man bakes bread, another sweeps the streets, another drives a cart, and another sits in an office and runs a business—all that would leave you none the wiser. These are facts, and yet you would not understand them. You could not comprehend them. That is my difficulty in trying to make you understand in a satisfactory way the life of this Blue Isle. I have to consider how to explain it. It is no use my telling you that one person sits by the sea all the time, weeping over her long-lost lover, another is in an alcoholic stupor, and another who retired years ago still thinks he is ringing the bells of his local chapel on Sunday, etc., etc.—that is not the whole picture of life on Earth or life on the Blue Isle; those are only bits of it—atoms of the whole. I do not want to particularize; I want to generalize with some detail. Therefore, I must say that if you were to pay this land a visit in your earthly bodies, as you are at present, you would be struck by the lack of excitement. You would think it was all so like the earth. That is what you would say to people on your return. "Oh, it's so much like our life here, only there are a lot of different races of mankind there."

Everyday life for the individual is strikingly like the everyday life he's always been used to. At first, he takes a great deal of rest; having the earthly habit of sleeping—and it is a necessity—he needs sleep here, too, for the present. We have no night as you have, but he sleeps and rests just the same. He has an interest in visiting different parts, exploring the land and its buildings, and studying its animal and vegetable life. He has friends to seek out and see. He has his pastimes to indulge in. He has his newfound desire for knowledge to feed.

The routine of a day here is similar to the routine of a day on earth; the difference is that earth's routine is often made by force of circumstance, whereas here it is made according to the desire for knowledge on this or that subject.

In clothing, we are all practically the same as on earth, and as there are so many races here, you can well understand that the general appearance of this land is most unusual and, in an odd way, particularly interesting and amusing, as well as instructive. I think I have said that, in general appearance, we are all as we were. We are only a very little way from Earth, and consequently, up to this time, we have not thrown off earthly ideas. We have gained some new ones but have as yet discarded a few or none.

The process of discarding is a gradual one. As we live here, we gain knowledge of many kinds and come to find so many things, hitherto thought essential, not only of no importance but something of a bore, a nuisance, and that is how we grow to a state of dropping all earthly habits. We get to the state of not desiring a smoke, not because we can't have it or think it's not right, but because the desire for it is not there. As with smoke, so with food, and so with many a dozen other things, we are just as satisfied without them. We do not miss them; if we did, we should have them, and we do have them until the desire is no longer there.

At first, there is practical freedom of thought and action, and there are only certain limitations imposed—not by rule but by conditions. Beyond these limitations, there is absolute freedom. After a time, when the spirit has advanced to the point of desiring knowledge and enlightenment, he will be drawn, like a piece of steel to a magnet, into contact with this or that house of organization dealing with the subject on which he desires knowledge. From the time of coming into contact with this house, the spirit will be, as it were, *at school.* He will surely have to attend this house of instruction. He will spend a good deal of his time there learning and, when finished with one house, will pass to another, but it is not compulsory information; it is craved-for information, and nothing is given until asked for. You are not forced to acquire anything. You are more than ever free agents. That is why, on earth, it is so essential to control your body with your mind and not the reverse. When you come here, your mind is all-powerful, and everything depends, for your own degree of happiness here, upon the kind of mind you bring with you.

The presence or absence of contentment is entirely due to the earthly life you have led, the character you have formed, the opportunities taken and lost, the motives of your actions, the help given, the manner of help received, your mental outlook, and your use and abuse of fleshly power. To sum all this up, it is the quality of mind control over the body versus body control over the mind. Mind matters, and body matters; it is entirely in your hands and is in whatever state you have made it in your life. On your arrival here, the degree of your happiness will be determined automatically by the demands of your mind.

When you are inclined to ask, "What are they all doing there?" Turn your mind to some dear one on earth who has taken up an out-of-the-way kind of life somewhere abroad, where you are not in constant and intimate contact, and ask yourself, "I wonder what he's doing now?" Then answer yourself by saying, "I suppose he's carrying on as usual." So are we, on the Blue Island.

~ Seven ~

INTIMATE LIFE

In Earth life, there is a good deal of reasoning and argument as to why we should do this or that—why we should refrain from many of the delights of everyday life and why we should take the straight and narrow path of self-righteousness. People say it is handicapping in their business or profession to have to observe these "nice points." They may not confess this thought openly, but to themselves they do—they do not see why such and such should not be done. True, they think it may injure so-and-so's business a little, but that is their affair.

All in ignorance. There is a reason, and that reason can be very easily found by applying the rule of common sense. I almost might call this a discourse on cause and effect. Earth life has deteriorated. The whole scheme of creation is planned with great precision, with the object of allowing free individual development and progress. Its rules are laid down clearly. Everyone knows by instinct when they are obeying and when they are disobeying these rules. They need no police officer to tell them. They may deceive themselves into thinking that such an act is all that it ought to be, but at the same time, they know in their own consciousness that that act or thought is not only *not* all that it ought to be, but that it is all that it ought *not* to be. I say that everyone knows, but almost everyone prefers to think they do not know.

Not one person on earth can stand up and say, I am not speaking a profound truth here! Mostly, these things are not considered from the point of view of right or wrong but from the view "Will I benefit from this?"—but I say that *all* people on earth *can choose*, and I do not say that they do, between good and not-so-good motives in their lives. Instinct does this for them. They cannot help themselves. They are bound to know. The trouble is that the vast majority, by force of habit and the desire for business gain, social gain, or any kind of gain, but always a gain for itself, has ceased to consider the quality of its actions and thinks only of the first result. It is a pity. It is more than that. Looking upon it from the next stage of evolution, it is PITIFUL. Poor, undeveloped egos are preparing their own discomfort and suffering—not hellfire but mental torture.

The self or spirit of an individual is encased in his or her mind, and, examined in a purely physical way, the brain is the most baffling organ of the body science has ever had to deal with. Much can be understood; all never will be. Judged as the casing and instrument of the soul, it becomes an even more delicate, intricate, and baffling piece of work. You all know that the mind is the generating house for all your acts and deeds, but you do not fully appreciate the fact that every act and every thought is recorded on the Ethers.

You do not see the elaborate scheme of work that goes on in any of your large business corporations when you buy something on credit. It is booked and passes through many hands before the bill is sent to you a little later, and once you pay the bill, you forget all about it, but that business corporation still has a record of it. So it is with the mind; an act or a thought, no matter what the quality, is recorded for all time. The settlement will come after physical life, and when you've paid, although the *book* is finished and troubles you no more, the record is still there. Now follow me. Thought is the force that drives and creates everything on Earth. Everything is mental before it becomes material. Every building was conceived mentally before being built.

Thoughts are divided into two different types: constructive and destructive. Thoughts referring to your meals, your clothes, and your appearance are not destructive until they are allowed to hinder the flow of constructive thought; when they do this, the character of these same thoughts changes and becomes destructive. It is the material embodiment of destructive thought that causes most of the distress and misery in the world. The sum total goes on increasing and will continue to increase until everyone, as a whole and individually, will listen and try to understand a little more about themselves beyond what is necessary for them to know, giving fuller play to the beneficent action of constructive thought, which alone can redeem and save the world.

~ Eight ~

MORE ABOUT INTIMATE LIFE

To a great extent, the individual hardships of earthly life are directly due to wrong thinking. I am fully aware that people are placed in many different positions right from birth. Some inherit unhappiness and difficulty from their parents, and their lot in life is harder and their pleasures are less than in the lives of those who are born in better conditions.

Accepting these differences of position and condition—one individual lives a life of much hard work, another a comfortable and perhaps rather idle life—the same rule of thought applies. The person who has grown up under hard conditions is, by circumstances, forced into a groove of thought—a regular rut. They cannot help themselves because there are no real attempts made by anyone to change their outlook; they may meet with material help from time to time, but they meet with little *practical* mental assistance. Because of their poverty thoughts, they add to their own difficulties instead of easing and finally removing them. The individual who is comfortably settled and has no particular worries has thoughts of abundance. They continue with the same positive thought processes. They are both building up their future mental states and experiences, which will carry over into the afterlife.

There are clever people of keen intelligence who use their brains to achieve material gain, no matter the cost to others. These people are indulging in the most destructive form of thought. They are not like the other two—one with destructive thought and the other with constructive thought. They are at once using destructive and constructive thought. The latter is entirely misapplied, and when they come here, the account against them will be much heavier because they will have built up a wall of greedy thought that they originally sent out and which they must settle in the afterlife.

A thought—no matter the heading it comes under—that has come into your mind that you have sent out is an accomplished thing so far as your *mind* goes. Your physical act may or may not keep swift accompaniment with the thought; that does not matter from the point of view of what you are building up for yourself *here.* Once you have had a thought, it is *done,* so far as your mind is concerned, and, whether you follow it up actively or not, you have to make repayment for it when you come here. I am not speaking about the thousand trivial thoughts of every hour, but about those that I might describe as being cemented as a belief.

You might say it is impossible to control every thought you have throughout the day. I agree that it is, but once you have accepted as fact what I have said, it would be wise to keep a sharp eye on your thoughts because they do matter. You may find this a very difficult concept to accept because it is indeed an intimate thing for each one; you do not know each other's thoughts while on earth, but every thought here is laid bare. In the afterlife, all thoughts are transparent, and there are no secrets.

~ Nine ~

FIRST ATTEMPTS

Leaving the question of time out of it entirely, as I must, I want to write about my first attempt to communicate with the people on Earth. I know there is much dissatisfaction with the spirit world on account of the practical impossibility of giving correct ideas related to timing. I would like to say a little about that before going into the main topic of today's writing. You must not be overly hasty in condemning us for this failure. On Earth, you all space your time by days, hours, etc., but those spacings are also based, or perhaps more definitely marked in your mental reckoning, on the habits of the day. You have always taken certain things at certain hours. You have a light sky and a dark sky; without a watch, you know fairly accurately the time of day by your inclinations—fatigue or freshness, the need for food or rest, etc., etc.

Now, on this side of the grave, we have no real necessity for rest or food. We have no dark sky, only a light one, and we have, for the sake of the present illustration, an unlimited supply of energy. Consequently, we are not able to break up time into spaces that correspond with earthly spacing. We do break up our time, but it is not the same as time as you know it; therefore, we can seldom be accurate in telling when a thing did or will happen. For that reason, I am not able to tell how long I had been in this country before I made my first attempt to link up with Earth again. To me,

I seemed to have lived in this land always. It appeared incredible to me that it had only been a few days since I arrived. I had not forgotten my family or my friends, but I felt peculiarly happy about them. I cannot think why, except that, finding my earth knowledge so very correct, I gathered strength in the feeling that they too would understand that everything was quite well with me and that this little delay in writing was natural considering the new country I had come to.

The house that is given over to this work on the Blue Island has been a regular haunting place of mine ever since my father told me of it, together with the other buildings. I went to this house a great deal and received much help from the various people in charge. They were all very sympathetic but entirely businesslike. It was not merely a house of tears and sympathy; it was an amazingly well-organized and business-like place. There were hundreds of people there. Those who had been on earth believed, and those who had not came to try to send a message home.

The heart call was the one that received the most serious attention. Many were there only as lookers-on, incredulous, and facetious. They got nothing more than the satisfaction of their own amazement. After a little time, my turn came.

For a building given over to this kind of work, it appeared to be inadequately equipped. I had rather expected to see many implements and instruments, many wires and machines, and the presence of electric forces, but there was nothing of that kind at all. It was all about the human element.

I had a long conversation with a man there—a man obviously of some importance, though I cannot say he looked like an angel; he appeared quite as mundane as myself. I had a long talk with him, and from him, I heard how a great deal of this work was carried on. He told me they had a system of travelers whose work was very close to the physical earth. They had the power of sensing people who could and would be used for this work at the earth's end. These individuals could locate and then tabulate the earth's people, marking each individual ability, and when the newly-arrived spirit came in search of help, these sensitives on earth were used as each could be used. This is a sketchy outline of the work done in that building. There I came frequently and tried to get my messages through to home by more than one means; I succeeded in some ways and failed in others. The spirit has much to do with himself and the success or failure attained; a great deal depends upon him. Every time I succeeded, I helped another. Every time I failed, I went for help and got it. Having given much time and study to the subject on earth, I was given unlimited assistance at this end of the line now that I needed it.

I want to explain how I got some of my first messages through and how I knew I had succeeded. We had been taught by this time how to come into close contact with the earth, although it was not possible for me to do this alone. I had a helper with me. I must call him an official. He came with me to my first trial.

We came into a room that seemed to have walls made of muslin—something and yet nothing. I knew it was a house and was conscious of the walls of the room, and yet they seemed such poor things because we could see through them and move through them. I could not have done this by myself at that time, but with my official, we did.

Then came the attempt. There were two or three people in this room, and they were all talking together about the horror of this great disaster and about the probability of people coming back. They were holding a seance, and my official showed me how to make my presence known. The controlling force, he told me, was thought. I had to visualize myself among these people in the flesh. Imagine I was standing there in the flesh, in the center of them, and then imagine myself still there with a strong light thrown upon me. Create the picture. Hold the visualization very deliberately and in detail, and keep it fixed in my mind that at that moment I *was* there and that they were conscious of me. I failed, of course, at first, but I know that after a few attempts I succeeded, and those people did actually see me. My face only, but that was because in my picture I had seen myself only as a face. I imagined the part they would recognize. I was also able to get a message through in precisely the same way. I stood by the most sensitive individual present, spoke, concentrated my mind on a short sentence, and repeated it with much emphasis and deliberation until I could hear part of it spoken by this person. I knew that, at last, I had succeeded. Many who did not have my earthly understanding of spirit communication received little, if any, impression from me at all.

There were no members of my own family present at that time. Had there been, it would have made it impossible for me, as I was then feeling their sorrow acutely, and I would not have been able to give my mind as much power as I did—I became almost impersonal. It was a good thing that my first attempt was purely a test to see if I could break through to home.

~ Ten ~

THE REALITY OF THOUGHT COMMUNICATION

In trying to establish a definite form of communication between the earth sphere and the Blue Island, people are always looking for the return of the physical part of the individual. They find it exceedingly difficult to accept even the most pressing mental tests as proof of communication, and in giving so much attention to this physical form, they nearly overlook the form of thought communication, which is much more personal and much less tainted by outside influence, such as the medium's mind, other sitters, antagonism, or bias either way. This form of communication is more real than is accepted by the majority of believers in its possibility.

In concentrating the mind on any one spirit person, you are sending out real, live, active forces. These forces pass through the air in precisely the same way that electric waves do, and they never miss their mark. You concentrate on Mr. A in the spirit world, and immediately Mr. A is conscious of a force coming to him. In this land, we are much more sensitive than while on earth, and when thoughts are directed to us by people on your side, we have a direct call from those currents of thought generated, and we are practically always able to come in close contact with the person who is thinking of us; when near and acclimatized to his conditions, we can impress thoughts and ideas upon his mind. He will seldom accept them for what they are but will think they are his own normal thoughts or something of a hallucination. Nevertheless, if frequent opportunities are given, he will be startled at the amount of information he can record. This applies to everyone, not merely to those who believe in these subjects. Anyone who sits for a moment and allows his mind to dwell on some dear one who has "died" will actually draw the spirit of that person to himself. He may be conscious or unconscious of the presence, but the presence is there.

If people on earth realized the result of their thoughts upon those whom they think about, they would be much more careful in giving their minds free play. There are so many thoughts possible, and some of them are concerns, but all of them affect the people they emanate toward.

Perhaps by telling you that all thoughts are recorded, I am making it more difficult for you to accept and understand. It would be better to explain that by "all thoughts," I mean all direct thoughts. In reality, every thought is registered on the ether. The personal ones are of no importance so long as they are not destructive thoughts.

In speaking of direct thought, I want you to understand that thoughts about other people, pleasant or unpleasant, are not thoughts of everyday trivialities.

Many people find it impossible to believe that every direct thought they have can influence or affect the person they are thinking about, but it's true. Frequently, the subject is not consciously aware of these thoughts that have been thrust upon him or her, but the influence is there in a greater or lesser degree of strength, and all these thoughts are very definitely registered in the conscious mind of the thinker and the subconscious mind of the subject long after the thought has passed.

When coming to this land, that whole record has to be dealt with. Not by a judge in wig and gown, but by our own spirit selves. In spirit life, we have full and clear remembrance of all these things, and according to the quality of these individual thoughts, we are brought into a state of regret, happiness, unhappiness, despair, or satisfaction. It is here that we meet with the desire to make a return, to put right all the discomfort and distress, minor or major, as the case may be, caused by thoughtless mind action while on earth.

This is why I say that while on earth, it is not only advisable but essential to keep your mind under control and in order. It is only wise to do so. The difficulty is that people will not realize this while on earth, although they know from their own inner consciousness that I am stating the truth.

I want you all to try to realize the results you are making, the unhappiness you are causing others, and the regret and sorrow you are laying up for yourselves in the next world when you have to face the conditions you have made. Remember that your minds are the generators. You are building up whatever is to be your next condition precisely by the lives you are leading on earth, by your thoughts, and by the degree to which your body controls your mind instead of your mind ruling supreme. So long as you are upon the earth, you are Body (Physical), Soul (Mind), and Spirit (Self). When you come here, you are Mind (Soul) and Self (Spirit) only. Therefore, for your own future happiness, it is essential that your mind rule during your earthly life. It is for you to say whether it will do so. If you are willing to pay your bill when you come over, carry on as you are, but there is no further credit given; you have to settle it here. If you are a quarter as practical as you all think you are, you will see to it that the mind leads. It can lead very delightfully, although you may think it leads only to religious restriction—it does not only lead there; it leads to all earth's pleasures and enjoyments, but it always holds the ruling hand and can stop at the right time, whereas the body cannot, and so it runs up debts that have to be paid, sometimes very dearly and bitterly.

The earth was made beautiful for Man to enjoy, not merely to tantalize him, lead him on, and then say, "No". That is not the way of our blessed Creator. He has given beauty and the faculty for enjoying beauty to all mankind, and so long as the mind rules, it will continue to be beautiful. But when only the body rules, influencing and degrading the mind as it will, then trouble lies ahead—much trouble and much acute regret.

When we are here, our minds work in the same manner; they obey the same rules, and the presence or absence of bodies does not hinder our thinking powers. Consequently, there is no difficulty in coming into contact with some of our people left behind and being in close contact with them, influencing them greatly, although many of them are unconscious of it. I want you to think of this and to realize that your own people can come to you, that thought is all-powerful, and that you can build up or destroy, help or hinder, draw near you or drive away from you, the people incarnate and discarnate, who were and who are so dear to each of you by this power of thought.

Thought communication is the closest link between the two worlds, but it must be well-ordered and well-trained. You must not imagine that every idea that enters your mind is put there by a spirit person; it is not so at all, but at the same time, if you train your mind in the way an athlete trains his body, you can then ask for and receive great knowledge and much help, both spiritual and material.

~ Eleven ~

IMPORTANT POINTS

A subject of this importance and interest is full of queries. Each one has his own questions to ask, and each brings what he considers a previously unnoticed point. I want, if possible, to answer a few of these constantly recurring questions now. I had many of these questions asked of me during my investigations while on Earth, and some of them I can finally answer at last. I want you first to realize that by the change of death, you *do not* become part of the Godhead *immediately.* The mysteries of life are not revealed to you as a kind of welcome gift on your arrival here. You must not think that I, or anyone else, has full knowledge on all subjects, profound and trivial, the moment we enter into spirit life. I may not be able to tell you when you will meet the love of your life, nor can I tell you when you will come into a fortune. I can only see a little farther than you, and I do not by any means possess the key to the door of All Knowledge and All Truth. We have each other to work for, and as we pass through one door, we find another in front of us to be unlocked, and then another, and another.

But, on the other hand, remember that I do know considerably more than you do because I am in more intimate touch with the Main Source of knowledge and have passed through an experience that is still ahead of you all. I would like to speak first about the word *conditions* and its true meaning. It is a word that is grossly misapplied in all forms of psychic work. It is given as a reason for this or that failure, for success, or for any peculiarity in result, and it is looked upon as necessary anywhere a seance is held. The main factor or element essential to obtaining good results lies more in the condition of the sitter's mind than in the room he is in. The mental attitude and the physical state of the sitter are more important than the presence of draped windows, thick carpets, exotic perfumes, etc. It is the method of mental approach that matters most. That is a feature often overlooked by even first-rate sensitives. Meta-physical props such as crystal balls, gemstones, mystical paintings, and symbols are not essential. However, a cheerful face, pleasant flowers, laughter, and a well-lit room are all helpful in uplifting the mood and increasing the vibration necessary for effective spirit communication.

Some people always try to ridicule communication with the next world, one of God's greatest blessings to mankind, and complain of what they consider to be senseless conditions ruling at a seance. As I have said, many of these conditions are meaningless and some-times a hindrance, but at the same time, others are necessary according to the kind of communication sought.

To make my point, I must recall to you how conditions govern everything, and so much everything depends upon given suitable conditions that people do not even notice that this is so. The simplest and perhaps most useful example of this is making a pot of tea. You must have the tea in a certain condition, and you must have the water in a certain condition—if you do not, you get poor results. Your flowers—you have your seeds in a certain condition of dryness, and you put them in the earth when the climate is in a certain condition, according to the time of year, and, once planted, you tend your plants, flowers, trees, everything according to the conditions they *demand.*

We demand conditions. Conditions govern the earth and all forms of life on it from an earlier state than that when conscious-ness begins—but I tell you, many of the conditions demanded by so-called intelligent spiritual workers in this subject are futile and —worse—harmful. You cannot achieve success in anything or along any line by directing your force in opposition to your intelligence. A vast number do so in this subject, and *that* is why there is so much failure. You may as well try to take a photograph without putting any film into the camera, and then when you get no result, you say the whole thing is impossible and fraudulent. You must have conditions in order to secure success in anything and everything. It is due to a lack of these necessary conditions that we sometimes fail to influence a person to do or not do a certain act. The spirit of a father may be fully conscious of his son contemplating a certain deed, such as suicide. Such knowledge will cause great sorrow to the father, and he will work to influence his son's thoughts in an effort to destroy his thoughts of suicide. However, because the son's obsession with suicide is so strong, he lacks receptivity, which prevents his father's ghostly influence from getting through, making the father powerless to intervene. Receptivity is, basically, the only condition required for spirit communication.

As spirits, we are free to visit other spheres. We are able to travel among these other lands, including the Earth. Thoughts about us sent out by people on Earth reach us. We sense from whom they come and can follow up with the person if we desire. We may not get thoughts from just anyone who happens to see our names and make a casual remark; however, anyone whom we were intimate with while on earth—a thought from them of us will come straight to us—as along a telephone wire from one house to another. We can come if we wish. In this way, we are able to help those left behind. We can influence them one way or the other, according to our idea of what is for their own good, but we cannot force an individual to commit certain acts or do impossible things for them, even for those dearest to us.

While on earth, one can give advice but cannot force it into practice—so here, we can influence but not coerce or create your life for you. Having attained this state, there is no parting, there is no sting to death, and we can still be with our loved ones on earth. Separation and parting are not known except by the law of attraction. We leave people behind on the earth who dutifully mourn for us and are genuinely upset at *their* loss, but after a while—short or long—their remembrance of us grows thin. They cease to think of us, to recall us, and to remember our companionship. In some cases, even those people come back into our lives when they themselves come to this land. Gradually, as they throw off the influences that dimmed their remembrance of us, they find the foundation of the old affection.

On the Blue Isle, you will not be continually associated with people who are not of interest to you. On earth, you eliminate, as far as is practical, the people who tire and try you, but here that can be done effectively because those feelings and instincts are entirely mutual. The governing force is love. Affections bind people together, and if the love between any two or any group is strong and genuine, then those people will be in close unison and happy together. But wherever love is not on both or all sides, there is automatically a falling away of the affected party. Nothing uneven or unequal holds here. When you come through death, you are attracted by people who share the same affection, and if you have an affection for another that is not equally shared, although you may be together at first, you will gradually cease to be in each other's company.

~ Twelve ~

THE STATE OF FREEDOM

While on the Blue Island, I studied, as all do, the secrets of self and life, and I came to realize the vastness of Creation. It is not life on earth and then life on this island only. As I progressed and put earth's inclinations aside, the desire for true knowledge rose up within me. My capacity for wisdom grew with the wisdom I acquired.

I learned of the existence of other lands besides this blue island, and eventually the time came when I was taken to these other spheres. I cannot tell you where they are, but it was like traveling among the stars. It seems as if my companions and I left our world and traveled through space until we reached another star and another land.

All races have the gift of free will and are free agents in determining their own destinies at all times, not only after the body's death. Just as the father and mother of a family order the day's routine for their children and allow the children to amuse themselves in their own way, so the human race is free to develop and model their lives upon their own individual patterns. All life is originally free; however, while on earth, people often believe they don't have free will—but they do. In the same way a loving father and mother influence and guide their children, we do our utmost to help and influence those we love who are still on earth. Love is the driving force that causes us to do our work.

We can be in close touch with our loved ones on earth, and through suggestions, we can influence them. Through our influence, great material goods can come to them. We cannot give material riches to anyone, but we can frequently give advice as to the best step to take in a business matter that, if taken, will bring them considerable material wealth. We can influence our loved ones in business the same way we influence them in other matters.

In saying we can and do influence people on Earth, I will not go into the precise process of how it works. It is enough to say that you know how you influence each other on Earth; here, the process is different, but the result is the same.

~ Thirteen ~

PREMONITIONS

There are many superstitions and reasons given to explain what is called a *premonition,* but the chief form of a premonition is that concerning the death of another. For instance, Mr. A has a premonition about the death of Mr. B. It is followed up later by an accident in which Mr. B is killed. The spirit friends who are interested in Mr. B have been constantly watching him; but they cannot make him do anything, they can only influence him one way or another. Now, all of the actions in Mr. B's life are producing certain effects, some of which Mr. B himself is not consciously aware of. His spirit friends can see a certain distance ahead and what the results of his actions will be, and although they will do their best to guide him, they cannot make him take the necessary steps to avoid his death. He sets his own destiny in motion, and he alone can alter it. At such a time, his spirit friends, realizing that he is in physical danger, will try to divert his actions and movements. Sometimes they are successful, but sometimes they are not, and Mr. B meets with his death. The thoughts being projected by his spirit friends have created a disturbance of thought force around him, and although Mr. B was not consciously aware of it himself, his friend Mr. A has subconsciously perceived the thoughts, which then manifested as a dream. When death premonitions do not come to pass, it is because spirit friends were able to influence and protect their charge.

~ Fourteen ~

RESIDENCE

I come now to the last days on the Blue Island and the taking up of our residence on the next, far more permanent world. Life on the Blue Island is transient; it's a land for acclimatizing the newcomer, and as soon as he's fit, he passes from it to what I might term the Real World, inasmuch as each one will be much longer on it than any has yet been on earth. We can, at will, return to the Blue Island, and many do so frequently, both to meet newly arrived friends and associates and to help any person or group with whom we are in sympathy. These are only visits, and we will never again return there to live.

Traveling here is a very different thing from the methods you all know, and we all set out in a large party for the Real World. Not our whole party, as on our first arrival; many weren't ready to leave, but with us were many other spirit people besides those with whom we had originally arrived. There was the same sensation of flying, moving rapidly through the air, and then we came to our new home. After the color and generally striking appearance of the Blue Island, this new land appeared less attractive at the outset. It was more toneless in color, and the people were more engrossed in their regular routine. It seemed as if we had returned to earthly life again. I think, on arrival here, we must all have been attracted to different parts of this land, for my own seemed strikingly like parts I had known on Earth, and there were also buildings I knew. Other people have told me the same, so I am confident that we are attracted to different parts of this new world in accordance with our preferences.

It is in this land that I and many other spirit people are and certainly will be in the future. We continue our studies and our work toward developing spiritually. We are all very conscious of each other in this land, and we continue life in a similar fashion to that we knew on Earth. We have our homes in the same way and our interests in other people, and according to taste, we cohabitate together in houses or on open hillside country. Some people live in very elaborate palaces, and it is very curious to note that many of these people led very rough and hard lives on Earth. Their idea of Heaven is a palace and a life of ease. After a period of time during which they must make specified progress in general development, these people are given their palaces in order to take full advantage of the environment and make forward steps in their evolution.

When we come to this land, we no longer desire food, drink, and sleep; we are now pure spirits in a rough state. There is still more refining to be done in this phase of spiritual life. There are Houses for Rest here as well as for Music, Scientific Research, and every kind of information and knowledge. The entrance fee for each of these Houses is Desire. We do not lead a life of continual cramming of information—we lead ordinary earthly lives but with a much keener social interest and much more freedom and exchange of thought. There is no distinction between the classes. Our earthly lives may be forgotten, as far as our individual tasks on earth are concerned, when those tasks are of little or no interest to us. It is only spiritual and mental knowledge and development that hinders and advances the individual here, and spirit knowledge is not hindered by whatever one's job on earth may have been. In this respect, there is a great and sudden broadening of the point of view of all comers to this land.

It is a land of freedom, happiness, and smiles brought about through genuine love for one another. It is impossible to over-emphasize the degree of freedom in this new world or the joy each and every person has in it. The form of life differs here enormously according to temperament, personality, and the influence of earthly life. People vary in strange contrast to one another. Many of us carry on with the same work as on Earth. Here, we have no need to work in order to obtain a daily livelihood; we work here solely for spiritual refinement and progress, and at the same time, we keep in touch with our earthly interests as a form of recreation.

We are not always, without any break, in one house or another studying this, that, and the other; we have a certain program to go through, but it has many breaks, and in this "off duty" time we come back to our dear people on earth, and either out of interest and love or from the desire to be useful, we try our utmost to help them in their material and mental difficulties.

We have every form of recreation here, as I have already told you when dealing with Blue Island. Any habit or hobby formed on earth can be indulged in here, always providing it is progressive. From this, you can understand that life after death is a very normal and natural affair. We still have our affections, and those that last are still strong, binding links. Between families and friends, we have the same affections—and yet not the same, because sometimes on earth there are differences that cause a silence between members of a family, and perhaps over here that family will once more be very united—the earth differences being based solely upon material things. Once the material and physical things are removed, the love often remains.

One great change that death brings is a much broader point of view and a much larger mind. A deeper understanding, a keener intuition, clears away immediately many former difficulties and misunderstandings. Once in this Real world and once past the first initiation, we are free to do as we wish, but we have to progress or we ourselves curtail our liberties. It is not enforced progress; we can take our own time about everything, but we must not allow any of the earth's instincts to increase in their power over us.

We can travel at will over our own world and over yours. So great is our speed and method of travel that we can be in two places almost simultaneously. Everywhere we go, we are conscious of our general love for one another. It is much more evident than on earth, and that great affection is the direct cause of the general brightness and radiance of this world.

~ Fifteen ~

GENERAL RESULTS

I have been away from my earthly life now for a number of years, and although I have been in constant and unbroken touch with my old conditions and affections, I have never, since leaving the Blue Island, had any desire to return to the earth for habitation.

There have been many occasions when I have wished I could talk by means of a physical tongue. With my extra sight, I know the right treatment when I see certain situations being mishandled. At such times, I have very badly wanted to return to earth for an hour in order to be the means of bringing about great improvements—beyond these passing desires, I have no wish to ever take up residence on earth again. My travels, work, and studies on this side of the grave are vitally important to me. Since being here, I have acquired greater knowledge and have been able to pass *some* of that knowledge on to people on Earth at different times.

Ever since I left the world—your world—I have been keenly interested in its development and very interested in its internal and external difficulties. Patriotism still holds with me, as it does with most of us, and will continue to hold so long as I have personal ties to the earth. When there are no longer any of these personal ties remaining, my interests will gradually and naturally turn more exclusively to *this* side among my own spirit people, and my place will be filled by another—and so it goes on, always moving forward, progressing, and evolving.

I have great satisfaction in seeing the advances I have made since my arrival on the Blue Isle. Initially, coming here was quite a shock to me. I had no idea that my death was so near when that particular year began, and I certainly had no desire that it should be soon. I had an overwhelming number of important things to take care of while on Earth. Soon after my arrival here, I quickly grew acclimated to the new conditions, the new appearance of everything, and the new power of locomotion and communication. We do not talk to each other very much here; we have a more expressive and intimate way than that. Here, without the need for vocal expression, we *can* talk in an earthly manner at will; however, every thought we have is heard without effort on our part. Every thought is transparent, and there are no secrets.

There are, of course, many vast differences between my world and yours, but I always find one of the most blessed and merciful differences between the two to be the manner in which the mental is unhindered by the physical. You on earth have mental desires and ambitions of various kinds, for money, success in business, pleasure, power, knowledge, etc.; but always these desires are limited, often made impossible owing to your physical condition—here, when the mental desire is good, the field is unlimited. Any mental desire for truth and knowledge, be it what it may, can be gratified in a most astonishing manner in *this* world. Be it good or bad, it will bring its results, and if the desire is bad, it will grow in power and must be paid for; if it is good, it will grow in power also and will bring strength and happiness with it.

You are now, while on earth, making your bodies for your next conditions. These are built up by your present lives and the quality of your thoughts. This world, which I have been in for a long time now, is the closest thing imaginable to your earth. It is full of minerals, vegetables, animals, and *all* forms of life. All the animals you have loved on earth and are educated to understand will be with you here. Those other animals who belong to no one in particular are here too, but they are in their own places. You may be saying to yourself, *Oh, then it is only a reflection of our word.* It is not that way—the earth is only a reflection of this world. Earth is not a lasting world. It is the training school. You are not only on earth to amass riches and enjoy life for what it is; you are there to learn the truth about your own character and how to control and develop it to make full use of all the earth's beauties and pleasures. But you must master the conditions on earth and not allow them to master you.

We spirit people have made great advances in our communications with Earth. We have been greatly and enormously helped by the physical strength of the spirits of all the young men and women who passed over during the recent fighting all over the world—not only English but all of them. They brought with them great physical power and determination, and we have been able, through this power, to break down many of the barriers that keep the two worlds apart.

Go alone in your imagination to the edge of a high cliff overlooking the sea on a warm and starry night. Stand there and meditate. Look down at the lights of the harbor, and then look up at the stars. You know where you are, and you are fully conscious of the flickering lights of the harbor and the stars. This is how we spirit people are: conscious of those left behind, some willing to wait, others fighting and struggling to make themselves heard. It is only a little way from Earth, and between our spirit state and the Great Universe, there is as much distance as between you on the cliff and the farthest star. We are only a little way along our journey—nothing has been forgotten. Love still remains.

~ Sixteen ~

THE GREAT ULTIMATE

I have explained to you that, as you are, so you will be when you come here. When you are here, you will qualify for a further state, which will be your lot in due time, and there you will be exactly as you have made yourself by your life *here.* Better or worse, happier or more unhappy. From there, you will go to a further state, another sphere, if you like, and there again, you will have made your own conditions.

In this further state, you will be more self-contained, a word I use to express a state of being less dependent upon other spirit people and knowledge for development and progress. In this sphere, you will again come into contact with your *whole record.* A record in full of all former states; and from this sphere, if your record has qualified to the point of allowing it, you will be given the choice of returning to earth again. Reincarnating—if your record does not qualify for *choice* in this matter, you will be *directed* either to return or to continue according to what the Teachers—the Purified Ones— consider will afford you the most opportunity for recreating or cleansing yourself in a necessary way. It is from this sphere that spirits return to Earth, but by the time the most advanced spirit has reached this state, they have forgotten in detail their association with Earth. I cannot give the shortest period of time that would be necessary to reach this sphere, but the sojourn in the Real World after the Blue Island is a much longer period than that of mortal life, and in each sphere, the sojourn is *longer*.

The spirits who have reached this "Return or Stay Sphere" pass to another altogether different and lighter land—and each becomes impersonal. Impersonal in the sense that they are no longer Jack Brown or Madge Black; they are now pure spirit people.

I have given a brief outline, sufficient for you to form your own ideas and your own mental pictures of Creation and its process. There would be no point in my going further into details because if I were to give the facts, you could not understand the conditions ruling in those advanced states. I am not able to fully understand them myself, for, as I have said, I am only a little way along on my journey.

Were I able to describe all the processes of our evolution, many would say, "Oh, but I don't want that!" But when progress has been made, intelligence has brightened, and reality is seen as Reality, not as Imagination, they will want it. If I told an old man in a wheelchair that he could have a motorcycle, he'd say he preferred his wheelchair, but if he were a young, robust boy of nineteen again, which do you suppose he'd choose? This is the underlying principle.

I have said that there are no partings. It is always possible and customary for spirits to keep in close touch with each other on this side. When the highest states of the impersonal are reached, there are no partings from dear ones; only a wider opening of that same door of love—a higher, purer love, a Golden or God love—to admit not one, two, or twenty but to embrace ALL.

~ Seventeen ~

CHRIST AND SPIRITUALISM

U nfortunately, the word *Spiritualism* has been associated with so many misconceptions that it affords scope for misinterpretation, and for this reason, thousands of people misunderstand the word and suppose that it deals only with forms of fortune-telling and chicanery of all kinds and must necessarily be wrong and dangerous— therefore the work of the anti-Christ. For this reason, it is a barred subject. Not only do these people know nothing about it, but they are so horrified at the travesty they have created that they would refuse to hear, see, or read a word about the subject. To all people who know Spiritualism, this attitude is tiresome and regrettable; nevertheless, it exists today in great force.

In my concluding chapter, I want to say a few simple words on this point. Spiritualism is not the work of Satan. All the teachings of Christ are to be found in the teachings of Spiritualism. Christ taught love amongst mankind, generous thought, and generous help for one another. "Love thy neighbor as thyself," and so on. Spiritualism teaches these same doctrines. Christ was imbued with the Divine Spirit, and He laid down laws upon which His disciples were to model their lives and their work, and in those laws, you will find the laws that govern Spiritualism.

Because one of the disciples was a dishonest, weak man, and because some of the workers since then, workers in the churches of

57

various and many creeds, have been and are to this day weak and sinful in their lives, you do not, any of you, think for one moment that the whole is evil. You realize that the teachings of Christ are the highest. Always, He spoke of Love as the binding link and the force of all good. I want you to understand, perhaps for the first time, that Spiritualism is based on the same foundations. All its creeds are rules given by Christ Himself. All the creeds existing on earth are based on these same rules.

It is for the individual to decide which particular creeds are most fitting for him or herself based on their beliefs. By their choice, they will show their ability to grasp the meaning of God's laws and, according to their own development, select the creeds they live by. Just as all roads may converge at a given point, so many creeds follow the main teachings of Christ. Some by narrow little roads and byways, some by wide roads, and some by main highways. Spiritualism is God's Main Highway.

THE END

Part Two: The World of Spirit

My Guided Tour of the Afterlife

The Essence of the Soul

Dimensions of the Spirit World

The Spirit World According to Swendenborg

Correspondence Between the Planes

Spiritualists Beliefs About the Afterlife

~ Eighteen ~

MY GUIDED TOUR OF THE AFTERLIFE

Behold I tell you a mystery: We shall not all sleep, but we shall all be changed—in a moment, in the twinkling of an eye, at the last trumpet. For the trumpet will sound, and the dead will be raised incorruptible, and we shall be changed.

1 Corinthians 15:51-52

The spirits have told me that their world is created and experienced through the application of two laws—the Law of Attraction and the Law of Manifestation. They explained that the Law of Attraction reflects back to us the energy we unintentionally project, while the Law of Manifestation reflects back to us the energy we intentionally project. Both laws are based on the concept that energy follows thought and applies to both the physical and spiritual realms of existence. Spirits can create whatever they want in the spirit world; all they have to do is think of what they want, and it will immediately manifest. They said that we can do the same thing in the physical world, but it takes longer.

During many of my mediumship readings, spirits have given me glimpses of their otherworldly environment. Most of the landscapes

I have been shown are beautiful earth-like vistas. Unfortunately, there have been a few occasions when I have witnessed dimly lit, gloomy-looking scenes. The spirits in these gloomy-looking vistas did not appear to be suffering. On the contrary, they seemed to be at home in their gloomy-looking surroundings. Out of all my glimpses of the spirit world, none could compare to what I witnessed during my guided tour of the afterlife.

One night, after going to bed, I asked Spirit (God) to show me the world of Spirit. As soon as I fell asleep, I began to dream. A man with an olive complexion and black hair approached me. He was dressed in a purple robe with a gold stole around his neck. A bluish-white light surrounded his head and body and emanated about three feet around him. This saintly-looking man introduced himself as Paolo—my tour guide, teacher, and fellow light worker. He took my hand and said that the world of spirit is created by thought, then proceeded to show me that world. This is what I dreamed of:

Immediately, I found myself thrown into total darkness, which swirled around me like an icy cold, black velvet blanket. I asked Paolo to explain why I was experiencing such a horrible, cold, and dark place. He told me it was the Abyss—a deep, dark pit in the lowest realm of hell where pure evil is cast into it and bound for all eternity. He told me not to worry; only entities that are of the purest evil reside in the pit. These entities include spiritual beings such as tulpas and golems, who were intentionally created by evil men to be spiritual servants, and demons, who were originally created by God to serve human beings but instead chose to rebel against God's creation. These demons despise mankind and are intent on wreaking havoc and causing destruction to the human race. The physical world belongs to human beings, and only human souls have the right to create in the earthly realm. Demons try to usurp this right by influencing people to commit evil deeds. Paolo said that human souls do not come here for eternity. Only the evil entities that worked through human souls to create destruction are sent here, while the human soul is eventually rescued and set free.

Next, I found myself walking along what seemed to be a dirt pathway. I was engulfed in a gray, misty fog that felt wet and cold. Once in a while, I could make out the silhouette of another human being or hear the sobbing of someone off in the distance. I asked Paolo where I was, and he said that I was in a realm of hell that extremely depressed souls go to immediately after death. I told him that I didn't think that was fair. He smiled at me and said that every one of these souls was there because of their own vibration and that they would only be there for a short period of time before being rescued and taken to the healing hospital in Paradise, which is also known as Summerland.

Almost immediately, I found myself standing in the middle of what looked like a huge hospital ward with rows of white metal hospital beds lined up on each side. The hospital ward looked different from any I had ever seen. It appeared to be a Grecian palace with no exterior or interior walls, only tall columns that extended from the floor to the ceiling all the way around the huge rectangular room. All types of beautiful, colorful mosaics are designed with glittering gemstones adorning the floor. The white gossamer draperies hanging between each column billowed in the breeze. The distinct scents of lavender, jasmine, and gardenias filled the air. I realized these were my favorite fragrances, and then it occurred to me that each soul here experiences the scents they enjoyed the most while in the physical realm. The spirit patients, who were dressed in white clothes, appeared to be socializing and conversing with one another. I heard a lot of joyous laughter and singing. I remember thinking to myself *what a drastic transformation these patients had experienced-from deep depression to complete and utter joy.* Paolo told me that most of the patients here were ready to be discharged to their new homes in a community of their choosing where they would find meaningful relationships and activities.

I asked Paolo to show me the communities. He took my hand, and suddenly I found myself in the middle of a beautiful garden surrounded by mansions of every architectural design imaginable. I looked around and noticed that each mansion had a pool, as well as a tennis and basketball court. Every type of flower, shrub, and tree imaginable existed in this garden, along with all kinds of birds, butterflies, buzzing bees (by the way, I was told the bees don't sting!), and all kinds of animals—big and small. Spirit people were everywhere. Some jogged and rode bikes through the park, while others took leisurely strolls or sat on benches made of gold while conversing with one another. I asked Paolo where God and the angels were. He said that God's throne and the angels exist in the celestial realm, which is two planes higher but close enough to provide bright light for Summerland. He explained that the countenance of the Creator is the light that illuminates the heavenly planes, where there is no darkness or night. Once again, he took me by the hand and whisked me away to another plane.

Instantly, we were standing in the courtyard of a grand palace. The courtyard was filled with marble statues of animals, fragrant flowers, shrubs, and trees of every variety. This place had the same grandeur as Summerland; however, whereas Summerland felt more like a plane of leisure, this plane felt like it was more about purposeful activity. I asked Paolo why this plane seemed to be a place of purposeful activity. He told me that we were on the plane of the Masters, who worked to create new worlds, heal old worlds, and intervene in special matters of existing worlds, such as the resolution of war and illness, so that races and species may survive. He said that we were standing in front of the Celestial Curia—the Great Senate House of the Universes.

We turned and walked up a few marble steps to the entrance of this grand building. Heavy doors that seemed to be made of solid gold automatically opened so we could enter. We were greeted by a tall humanoid entity with six wings who was dressed in a white robe with a silver sash around his waist. His feet were clad in sandals that matched the color of his sash. He introduced himself to me as Seraphiel, a security guard in the order of the Seraphim.

He acknowledged and embraced Paolo with a hug and said, "Welcome, St. Paul; it's good to have you back. I know you have been busy with many special assignments, but the council of Elohim will be expecting you to take your seat soon for a vote on the next phase of creation."

I looked at St. Paul in amazement and thought to myself, *Is this the St. Paul of the New Testament?* He heard my thought and replied, "Yes, It is I. Also known as Saul, and known by you as Paolo. We must hurry now; we have one more plane to visit." He took my hand, and for the final time, we were on our way to another dimension.

Immediately, I found myself riding on a fluffy white cloud with Paolo. We seemed to be ascending higher and higher. Beautiful angelic-looking beings were riding up and down on their own cloud as if on an elevator, as well as fairy-like beings who flapped their wings to move about through the air. I asked Paolo where we were going. He told me that we were on our way to the throne of God, also known as the Spirit of All Creation. The light emanating from the throne seemed to get brighter as we rose higher, but it didn't hurt my eyes. In the background, I heard a symphony playing classical music. Periodically, I also heard what sounded like thunder. I asked Paolo why there was thunder in heaven. He said that it was the voice of the Creator. We finally stepped off our cloud and onto what looked like a sea of glass. I looked up and saw many structures that looked like cathedrals made of crystal. In the center of these cathedrals was a huge throne made of solid gold and embellished with fine gemstones. Sitting on the throne was a huge ball of brilliant light. This ball of light contained seven different faces. I thought to myself, *These must be the faces of the seven spirits of God.* Behind the main throne of God were twenty-four slightly smaller thrones. I asked Paolo why there were other thrones. He said that the other thrones belong to the Elohim—the senators of the Celestial Curia—who sit upon these thrones when it is time to create or intervene in matters of the Universes. I told Paolo that I had been taught in church that God's throne was the only throne in heaven. He laughed and said, Together we are the Elohim; we are one with God, including you, and God is one with us. Suddenly I remembered the following verses found in John 17:22-23 of the International Standard Bible:

> *I have given them the glory that you gave me, so that they may be one, just as we are one. I am in them, and you are in me. May they be completely one, so that the world may know that you sent me and that you have loved them as you loved me.*

I asked Paolo if God or the Elohim decided on the judgment of mankind. He said that God doesn't anyone to heaven or hell. That decision is made by each individual in accordance with their state of consciousness, belief in grace, and the Law of Attraction. The Law of Attraction basically states that like attracts like. If your state of consciousness is one in which you are feeling happy, enthusiastic, and appreciative, then you are sending out positive energy. On the other hand, if you are feeling anxious, stressed out, angry, resentful, or sad, you are sending out negative energy. If you believe in grace, then you will receive grace for any actions you took in earthly life that you don't feel good about. Source energy (God) responds enthusiastically to your vibrations. It doesn't decide which one is better for you; like a mirror, it reflects back to you the image of the energy you are emitting, so you get more of what you're putting out.

Then I asked him how people could be rescued from lower vibrational frequencies. He said that when a soul calls out for help, it will receive grace. Grace is the energy that raises a soul's vibration and sets them free. The Master, Christ, descended to earth to teach and embody the energy of grace. He is one of the Elohim who sits on the throne.

After this last reply, I remember waking up feeling extremely overwhelmed by what I had just seen and heard. I looked over at my alarm clock, and the digital face of the clock read 1:11. It was then that I realized I actually had a spiritual encounter, not just a dream. I thought to myself, *Three ones, really? Three is the number of the Holy Trinity—one in three and three in one. Wow!*

~ Nineteen ~

THE ESSENCE OF THE SOUL

The Essence of the Soul is Divine Consciousness.

—*Shiva Negi*

Death is simply the separation of the soul, or spirit, from the physical body. I prefer to use the word soul because I think it connotes the total essence of an individual spirit person. While still connected to the physical body, the etheric layer of the soul acts as a power source for the physical frame, thereby animating it with vital life force energy. When this power source, or etheric layer, completely separates from the physical body, the soul is freed, and the physical body begins to perish.

According to many Eastern religious and spiritual philosophies, such as Hinduism, Buddhism, and Jainism, the soul is comprised of at least seven subtle bodies, which are layers of energy that are part of and extend beyond the physical body. These layers, or subtle bodies, form an integrated system, which makes it possible for us to access higher multidimensional planes of consciousness, whether the soul is in or out of the physical body. There is quite a bit of variation in the popular literature concerning the actual number and categories of these subtle bodies, which can be very confusing;

therefore, I will present what I feel is an accurate depiction of the soul.

Instead of thinking in terms of the soul being made up of different subtle bodies, I like to think of these subtle bodies as being characteristics of one soul body; therefore, for the sake of simplicity, I will not treat the subtle bodies as if they exist on their own, because I don't believe they do. With the exception of the etheric body, I will treat the subtle bodies as aspects of one astral body. The astral body, which is composed of pure conscious energy, carries the core essence of who we are, such as our personality, intellect, desires, likes, and dislikes. This body continues to exist even after the death of the physical body.

There is a special layer known as the etheric body, which seems to have a function that is uniquely different from the other bodies—it acts as a powerhouse of energy, which I believe animates the physical body while alive and the astral body after death. The etheric body, which is an exact replica of the physical body, links the physical body to the soul. Life-giving energy from the Creator, known as Prana, is drawn in through the etheric body and distributed to the physical body. Prana, which is found in all living things, is the Sanskrit word for this vital force. Known as Chi in Chinese, Ki in Japanese, and Mana in Polynesia, Prana has a consciousness of its own.

I believe the etheric body feeds the astral body with sustaining energy after the physical body dies. Physical death occurs when the cord connecting the ethereal body to the physical body is completely severed. Many people who astrally project have reported seeing this cord and described it as being a silvery-white rope that attached their ethereal body to their physical body via the navel or head. I did not witness this cord during any of my out-of-body episodes. I was so caught up in each of my experiences that I was oblivious to how I was connected to my physical body. As an interesting side note, it's the ethereal body that energy healers work on to affect healing in the physical body.

~ Twenty ~

DIMENSIONS OF THE SPIRIT WORLD

Death is no more than passing from one room into another. But there's a difference for me, you know. Because in that other room, I shall be able to see.

—Helen Keller

All spiritual beliefs state that our soul goes somewhere after death—but where? In this section, I will briefly explain theories on the nature of the spiritual realms, which man may go to after death, as postulated in the doctrines of Theosophy, Swendenborgism, and Spiritualism. Then I will discuss what the spirits have revealed to me about their world.

Theosophists believe the soul is the center of individualized consciousness within the all-consciousness of the Universal Mind, and its latent God-like attributes are expressed through a mechanism of consciousness that is formed of the matter of the various spiritual planes. Seven primary planes with many sub-planes have been identified in theosophical literature. For the sake of simplicity, I will omit the physical plane and categorize the spiritual realms into five planes. I will also divide the astral realm into two sub-planes.

In Theosophy, the ethereal plane is the first realm of the spiritual dimensions. I like to think of the ethereal plane as being in the "real-time zone" because it is a direct and objective reflection of physical reality in real-time with some properties of the astral dimension, such as a fluid landscape that is permeable. This real-time zone overlays and permeates the physical dimension and contains a perfect reflection of reality within it. Everything happens in real-time, as reality actually happens. Out-of-body projectors traveling within the real-time zone will perceive themselves as following the actual spatial contours of the physical world but with the ability to fly and pass through solid physical structures. Projectors can also travel anywhere in the physical universe at will, at any speed, just by expressing their intent through thought. The experience is much like being a ghost because the Newtonian laws of physics do not apply. At the time of this writing, I have experienced this plane of existence twice during spontaneous out-of-body projections.

The second spiritual plane is the astral plane. Unlike the ethereal plane, the astral plane is completely nonphysical. Although the astral plane consists of many different realms and layers within those realms, I believe it can be divided into two main realms—the lower and higher realms. Each layer within these realms vibrates at a different frequency, with the lower levels vibrating at the lowest frequency and the upper levels vibrating at the highest frequency.

Between the ethereal and lower astral realms is a layer known as the abyss, which acts as a veil to conceal and separate the ethereal realm from the lower astral realm. This veil keeps spirits from the lower astral realm from moving down into the ethereal plane; however, higher beings can come down through it.

Hell was not intended for human souls, but most souls who find themselves in the lower astral realm upon death are usually filled with the same negative beliefs, emotions, thoughts, and feelings they had in physical life. The Law of attraction can draw situations and circumstances into our spiritual life just as it does in earthly life; however, anything we manifest by the law of attraction while in the spiritual realm will manifest quicker than it would if we were in the physical realm. Based on our beliefs, extremely low-frequency aspects of our conscious mind are responsible for manifesting our experience in the afterlife.

The Lower Astral Realm

The lower astral realm may have very low light in some places and be completely devoid of light in others. This realm is also home to negative entities such as thought forms called tulpas, servitors called golems who were created by man, and fallen angels called demons who were created by God but fell from grace. These entities are grounded in this realm because of their low frequency.

Unlike a created entity or thought form, a soul in this realm will eventually rise from the lower astral plane to the higher astral plane by raising its vibration. Souls can raise their vibration to a higher frequency by coming to an understanding of their human side and why they committed certain acts. They finally enter a state of grace when they choose to love and forgive themselves for those acts. The hellish realms were never intended for the human soul. If a soul ends up there, it's because they are in a negative and destructive state of mind. The loving Creator offers love and grace to all who will accept it, but we must choose to allow ourselves to receive this love and grace by loving and forgiving ourselves.

As I write this section, I am reminded of a forty-seven-year-old male patient of mine who died from a heart attack while in our emergency department (ED); fortunately, they were able to resuscitate him. He was admitted to the cardiac step-down unit, where I was assigned to do his pre-op teaching as well as the prep for his CABG (Coronary Artery Bypass Graft) surgery scheduled later that afternoon. As I hung his IV antibiotic, he told me about the after-death experience he had while in the ED. I will not recount his whole horrifying experience here. Instead, I will sum it up in his own words: "When I died in the emergency room, I went to hell but was rescued by Jesus." His story was unlike any other I have ever heard from my patients. To him, hell was a real and horrifying place, but he knew in his heart that he didn't belong there. No human soul does! (You can find the complete story in my second book, *My Adventures as a Psychic Nurse & Medium: Haunted Hospitals.*)

It becomes easier to love and forgive ourselves when we acknowledge how our lower, or shadow selves, can take control of and dominate our higher, divine selves. Like Christ, we are fully human and fully divine. Praying for our loved ones in Spirit is another way to help them raise their vibration, regardless of the plane they find themselves on. Communicating love and forgiveness to them is very comforting and therapeutic for them and for us.

The Higher Astral Plane

The landscape of this plane is a lot like Earth's. The astral plane is where our consciousness resides between lifetimes. How we experience this realm (or any realm) depends upon our state of mind prior to death and the beliefs we have about life after death. All of the astral plane is highly connected to emotional energy and can even be shaped by it. This realm is what Christians refer to as Paradise, and Spiritualists refer to it as Summerland.

A soul who passes into the middle astral plane upon death is met by friends and loved ones. Those with strong religious beliefs will be met by the religious figures of their religion. They will also be grouped with other souls who hold the same religious beliefs.

The Messianic Plane

Like Summerland, this realm is also a joyful place with beautiful earth-like vistas. The vibration here is much greater—there is a strong emotional perception of love and being one with God while still perceiving yourself as an individual spark of God. In this realm, you understand the unity of all things and recognize that love for another is actually love for yourself. Jesus taught from this plane.

The Celestial Plane

This is the plane where the entire universe connects at the energy level. The confines of the soul no longer exist, and you are connected to everything. It is a place of pure beauty, bliss, freedom, and unity. It is the seat of the Creator and the center of all creation.

The Akasha Plane

Akasha is a Hindu word that can be translated as sky, space, or ether. It is the space that fills the sky and connects everything within it. It could easily be referred to as the matrix of the universe. The Akasha plane does not exist in any single specified space; it exists within and around everything.

Ether is the air-filling substance that pervades the akasha and acts as a medium of transmission, or communication. Considered the first natural element in Hindu philosophy, it gives birth to the other elements—earth, air, fire, and water. It is the substance, or mana, that provides the template for physical form and is connected with the power behind all creation. This substance is the force behind every magical performance, religious or profane.

The Hall of Records exists on this plane. Originally called the Book of Life, it has also been referred to as the holographic archive of the universe. It contains a record of every event that has occurred in the physical world since its inception. In addition to past records, the akasha is said to contain the imprint of present and future memories.

~ Twenty-One ~

THE SPIRIT WORLD ACCORDING
TO SWEDENBORG

God created us in such a way that our inner self is in the spiritual world and our outer self is in the physical world. This was so that the spiritual part of us, which belongs in heaven, could be planted in the physical part the way a seed is planted in the ground.

—Emanuel Swendenborg

Emanuel Swedenborg—a 16th-century scientist, Christian mystic, theologian, and philosopher—describes creation as being made up of two separate but coexisting worlds: the natural world and the spiritual world. The natural world includes everything you see while in your physical body—trees, grass, flowers, the sky, houses, other people, your own body, and so forth. The spiritual world consists of unseen realities like heaven, hell, and the world of spirits in between. Swendenborgians believe that all human beings arrive in the spirit world as equals, regardless of their religious background, personal beliefs, nationality, gender, or race.

In the spirit world, we have bodies, live in houses, enjoy community life, and are surrounded by plants, animals, and vistas like those on Earth. However, things work differently in the spiritual world. What we see is determined by what we are thinking. Individuals and places are only as near or as far away as our thoughts of them. Thinking of a person or place can actually take you there. While the spirit world might not seem very different from the natural world at first glance, it is actually a realm where our inner state of being (consciousness) is reflected in our surroundings.

When people first enter the spirit world, they are often greeted by friends or relatives who crossed over before them. Spouses may be reunited, although not necessarily forever. Divorces are made in heaven as well as on earth. If two people were truly twin flames on earth, they may choose to live together as spouses in heaven too. Those who did not find love on earth will eventually find their perfect match in heaven—no one is ever alone unless they wish to be.

Swedenborg referred to the realm we enter immediately after death as the world of spirits. This is an intermediate realm situated between heaven and hell and can be thought of as a "sorting out" zone from which spirits either go to heaven or hell. The Theosophist named this realm Summerland; however, it is also recognized as the place of the afterlife among Wiccans and other earth-based pagan religions. Swedenborg described three states of consciousness that people might pass through in this realm.

In the first state, people are essentially the same as they were in life. They have all of their memories, beliefs, and attitudes toward things, and they may even manifest the same surroundings that they had on Earth. Swedenborg states that this is why some people who have died aren't even aware they are in the spirit world and may try to deny it if they are told that their physical body is dead. The spirit world is a place where a person's inner nature becomes the whole of their being. This first state might last anywhere from a few hours to a year or more, depending on how long it takes for a person's outer nature (what they outwardly say and do) to harmonize with their inner nature (what they truly feel and believe). Anyone who has become totally transparent in this life, whether transparently loving or transparently hateful, is fully ready for either heaven or hell and goes straight in.

In the second state after death, a soul becomes aware of the deeper parts of their inner nature. They act according to their inner values and are drawn to souls of like character. No "judge" passes sentences of guilt or innocence—we seek kindred spirits because that is where we feel at home.

There is a third state for people who are ready to go to heaven. It is a time for learning about heaven and how to lead a life that allows one to experience it. By this time, the soul is already in touch with the community in heaven, where they will ultimately live, but may still have a lot to learn about their new community.

Swedenborg teaches that we are surrounded by the world of spirits, with heaven above us and hell below us; those in the highest heaven are closest to the Lord, while those in the lowest hell are described as being farthest away. Swedenborg described the Lord—who exists at the top of everything—as a living sun radiating divine good and truth throughout creation. While Swedenborg describes heaven as being a place of inexpressible joy and peace, he also states that people who are not ready to experience a certain level of heaven will feel uncomfortable, even sick, and will be forced to retreat back down to lower levels until they have been properly prepared.

According to Swedenborg, hell is the part of creation that is farthest from the Lord. Hell has different regions and levels, just as Heaven does. Since the Lord is the source of light and heat in the spirit world, the deepest hells are also the darkest and coldest because they are the farthest from God. The only light and warmth that exist in hell arise from the fires of malice that emanate from its inhabitants. Souls who live in the deepest hells are the ones who embrace evil on the innermost levels of their being and find great delight in inflicting pain on others.

The popular Christian image of hell is one of fiery torment—a pit into which God casts sinners as punishment for their sins. The picture that Swedenborg paints is very different. He states that God does not judge or condemn anyone to hell to punish them. Also, there is no Devil who tortures sinners. It is the people in hell who torture each other by lying, manipulating, and inflicting pain, as they did when they were alive.

~ Twenty-Two ~

CORRESPONDENCE BETWEEN
THE PLANES

As above, so below; As below, so above.

—The Kybalion

Hermeticism is a philosophical system that is based on the teachings of Hermes Trismegistus. Long before the days of Moses, Hermes Trismegistus, who is considered the master of esoteric knowledge, taught the "Hidden Wisdom" known as Hermetic philosophy. One of the concepts taught in this philosophy is called the Law of Correspondence. This law states that there is harmony, agreement, and correspondence between the planes of manifestation. All that is included in the Universe emanates from the same source, and the same laws, principles, and characteristics apply to each plane, or level, as each manifests its own phenomena on its own plane.

The Law of Correspondence According to Theosophy

In *The Secret Doctrine*, Blavatsky wrote about the Law of Correspondence. This law, as noted in the Kybalion (a book published in 1908 on the Hermetic Philosophy of Ancient Egypt and Greece), states that the world above is the same as the world below and that the world below is the same as the world above. In other words, the physical world (microcosm) is a miniature copy of the spiritual world (macrocosm). Through the Law of Correspondence, a theosophist seeks to discover the first principles underlying various phenomena by finding a shared idea.

The Law of Correspondence According to Swendenborgism

All things that exist in the earthly world and its three kingdoms—animal, vegetable, and mineral—correspond to those things in heaven. Every single one of our physical universes has a corresponding spiritual universe in heaven. That is, the things in the natural world correspond to the spiritual world because the natural world springs forth and subsists from the spiritual world. Both worlds emanate and subsist from the creative power of the Divine Mind, which, if separated from it, would perish and disappear. Every aspect of our earthly lives has a correspondence in Heaven. We are able to talk to our loved ones in heaven because of the correspondence of communication.

As all things that are in accord with Divine order correspond to heaven, so all things contrary to Divine order correspond to hell. All things that correspond to heaven have a relation to good and truth, but those that correspond to hell have a relation to evil and falsity.

~ Twenty-Three ~

SPIRITUALIST BELIEFS ABOUT
THE AFTERLIFE

Spiritualism is the Science, Philosophy, and Religion of continuous life based upon the demonstrated fact of communication, by means of mediumship, with those who live in the Spirit World.

—*The Fundamentals of Spiritualism (Rev Ed. 2002).*

Spiritualists believe that God is the formless, Infinite Intelligence that created the universe and is present in all things. It is the dynamic force behind our world as well as other worlds. God's purpose is creation and progression, with the ultimate reward of life being seen not here on earth but in the higher planes of spiritual existence.

They also believe that when we make our transition into the realm of Spirit, we leave our physical form behind; however, our personality survives this, and we continue to exist on the spiritual planes. We are still who we were in physical life but without physical bodies. Heaven and Hell are not places to which we are destined to go, but states of mind of our own creation. Our place in the world of Spirit is determined by the Universal Law of Attraction, as our thoughts, words, and deeds determine where we will be. In other words, we make our own Heaven or Hell by virtue of our thoughts, words, and actions.

Spiritualists do not believe in the devil. They believe some souls have encased themselves in their own negative persona to the point where they find themselves on the hellish plane and must cleanse themselves of lower vibrational thought in order to rise to a higher plane. There is no eternal damnation because there is no absolute evil that can separate us from the Creator. Further, they do not believe in a vindictive God sitting in judgment over us. We are our own judge and will receive compensation or retribution for whatever we have done, whether good or bad; however, we are given the opportunity to make spiritual progress and undo any wrongs we committed while on earth. Spiritualists believe that we continue to grow and progress after we make our transition, as long as we choose to pursue growth. There is always more development open for us if we choose it.

About Shirley Smolko

S hirley Smolko, also known as *The Venetian Medium*, is a natural Psychic Medium, which means she was born with the ability to perceive psychic information and communicate with the souls of people that have passed away. In addition to being a Psychic Medium, she is a publisher, author, and lecturer.

She holds a Bachelor of Science in Nursing, a Master's in Business Administration, and another Master's degree in the Science of Accounting. She is also certified in grief counseling.

Shirley lives in the USA with her husband, Joe, and their two cats—Zoey and Cecilia. You can find out more about Shirley, her books, and what she is up to by going to: venetianmedium.com, or cavallaropub.com.

Books By Shirley Smolko (As Of This Printing):

- *My Adventures as a Psychic Nurse & Medium: Spirits Everywhere!* (Previously published as *Adventures of a Psychic Nurse: Spirits Everywhere!*)
- *My Adventures as a Psychic Nurse & Medium: Haunted Hospital!* (Previously published as *More Adventures of a Psychic Nurse: Haunted Hospitals!*)
- *Just a Thought Away: Communicating With Loved Ones In Spirit*
- *Money Wants Me!*
- *Money at Your Command!*
- *Secret to the Science of Getting Rich*
- *At Your Command!*
- *Revelations of the Afterlife: A New Arrival*
- *Wisdom From the Wealthy Dead: A Medium Interviews the Souls of Three American Tycoons*

BE SURE TO LOOK FOR MORE BOOKS TO COME!

ABOUT W. T. STEAD

William Thomas Stead was born July 5, 1849, and perished in the sinking of the Titanic on April 15, 1912. He was a British newspaper editor and pioneer of investigative journalism. Stead published a series of hugely influential campaigns while acting as editor of *The Pall Mall Gazette*, and is best known for his 1885 series of articles, *The Maiden Tribute of Modern Babylon*. These were written in support of a bill, later called the "Stead Act" which raised the age of consent from 13 to 16 years of age.

His style of "new journalism" paved the way for modern tabloids in Great Britain. He has often been referred to as "the most famous journalist in the British Empire" because he revolutionized how the press could be used to influence public opinion and government policy. He was a respected and well-known reporter on social issues such as child welfare, legislation, and the reformation of England's criminal codes.

At the request of President William Taft, Snead boarded the Titanic to take part in a peace congress at Carnegie Hall. According to the eye witness of several survivors, Stead helped several women and children into the lifeboats and gave his life jacket to another passenger. A later sighting of Stead, by survivor Philip Mock, witnessed him clinging to a raft with John Jacob Astor IV. "Their feet became frozen", reported Mock, "and they were compelled to release their hold; both of them drowned."